How I Teach Welding:

Professional Advice on

Implementing a Welding Program

Scottie Smith

Published by Agreement with Summerfield Publishing,
New Plains Press
PO Box 1946
Auburn, AL 36831-1946

ISBN:
978-0-9986857-7-9

Library of Congress Control Number:
2019934429

Smith, Scottie 1971 –

Cataloging in Publication Data
Technical Manual: Welding Instruction Program Development

Title:
How I Teach Welding:
Professional Advice on Implementing a Welding Program

Our thanks goes out to Northwest Florida State College for allowing the publication of the photographs in this book.

HOW I TEACH WELDING:

PROFESSIONAL ADVICE ON IMPLEMENTING A WELDING PROGRAM

Scottie Smith

Dedication

I would like to dedicate this book to my family: to my wife Kim, who has supported me whole-heartedly throughout my journey, to my daughter Kelsea, and to my son Wesley, who have both endured through my numerous welding stories, and to my mother Donna, who taught me not to be afraid of failure and to always try my hardest at everything I do. And finally, to my father Frank, who gave to me the love I have for welding. He truly is my hero. I miss you, Paps!

Table of Contents

Chapter 1

My Philosophy

Purpose of Training and Education

What is the purpose of training and education? The purpose of any training or education is to teach a person a new skill or give them new information that they can use to improve their performance at a task or improve their personal situation. The purpose of weld training, at the technical school or college level, is to give someone the skills necessary to find employment. That job should help them improve their personal situation by increasing the money they make. Simply put, the main point of weld training is to give the student the necessary skills to get a job. That is it. It is not about making the person a more well-rounded individual. It is about them getting a better job than the one they had when they started the training. I believe too many schools and colleges have forgotten this and they want to make students "well-rounded" by requiring students to take classes that do not relate to employment. These classes have nothing to do with the job for which a person is trained. Weld training is about making someone job ready! Period!

The best way to get someone job ready in welding is for the weld training to emulate a job setting. And that is my philosophy–make the weld training reflect industry standards and policies as much as possible, so that the students will be ready for employment when they complete the welding program. Every time I think of adding a new element to my program or shop, my first thought is "Is this how it is done in industry?" or "Will this new element help my students be job ready or help them get a job?" If the answer is no, to either of those questions, then I do not add the new element.

Quality over Quantity

I believe in quality over quantity when it comes to students. What do I mean by this? I would rather have 12 highly motivated and dedicated students that are serious about being professional welders than have 30 students that are only mildly interested in being welders and are taking the welding classes so they can say to their parents that they are in school. Most school administrators would rather have the numbers, but quality will bring quantity. Let me explain.

In education, the number of students equals money. The more students a school has and the more classes the students are enrolled in, the more money the school receives from federal and state governments. Just recently the number of graduates in comparison to the number of students has become a factor in calculating funding dollars. But the main factor in deciding funding dollars is the number of students. So, almost all school administrators want the seats filled. Not many administrators are concerned with the quality of the students in the programs. They are concerned more with the number of students in the program.

In my experience, if you get a few quality students that are serious about being professional welders graduating from your program and these students are successful, they will bring in more quality students. These few students will spread the word and the next year you will have a few more quality students, and the next year even more. So that in few years, your program will be filled with almost all quality students and you will have the numbers the administration wants. You cannot build a quality program with sub-quality students. Garbage in, garbage out!

How do I get quality students? One of the main things I do to ensure my program attracts quality students is requiring that each potential student pass a drug test for admission into the welding program. Anyone interested in attending my welding program is required to pass a 10-panel urinalysis drug screening to get onto the admissions list. I have copied the testing system the nursing program at my college uses. We use the My Student Check system (https://candidate.precheck.com/StudentCheck). This is a national system of collection sites and testing labs. So, no matter the state in which you reside or in which you teach, you should be able to use this system. The prospective students log into the website and set up a profile. In the profile, they ask for the students' zip codes. The website will direct the students to the nearest collection clinic and it even sets up the appointments for the potential students. The students pay for this drug screen out of their own pockets. Currently, the drug screening cost is $46 in my state. The cost gives the students some skin in the game right at the beginning. This step helps ensure that potential students are serious about learning to weld. It also helps weed out unemployable students and makes students more attractive to employers because the employers know that my students have had to pass a drug screening test.

I know this makes me sound like an elitist, unconcerned about the majority of students that want to learn to weld. I am not an elitist. I believe that any person that wants to learn to weld should have the opportunity to learn to weld. I just want them to know that if they come to my program that they had better be serious because I am serious. And they should know that I demand the best out of my students because my students will be the best! If someone cannot cut it, they fail out and move on to a different program.

I believe my program is the Harvard of welding schools. Harvard University is one of the most demanding universities in the world. Only the best and brightest get into Harvard and only the best of the best graduate from Harvard. That is how I see my welding program. Only the best and brightest get in and only the best of the best graduate. But the ones that do graduate have the highest skills possible coming out of a welding school and the opportunity for a great welding career.

You can't teach what you don't know.

It seems that a lot of welding instructors today are trying to "Fake it until they make it." And you cannot do that as a welding instructor. You cannot teach what you do not know. I personally do not have any experience in the aerospace field, so I do not teach welding techniques used in the aerospace industry. Some people would say that I am short-changing my students by not at least exposing them to aerospace welding, but I don't want to lie to my students by teaching them wrong techniques that would make them ill-prepared if they used those techniques, someday. Plus, there is not a job market for aerospace welding in the area where I am located, so why waste limited training time on a welding technique that is not in demand in my area?

I teach what I know. I know construction pipe welding. Once I have taught my students the fundamentals of welding: striking an arc, correct travel speed, bead size, and bead placement–on steel plate, I push my students to pipe. I have my students do as much practicing on pipe as possible, as early as possible, because pipe welding currently has the largest demand for welders and pays the highest wages. And pipe welding is what I know. I teach what I know. Teaching what you know also helps you focus your welding program. All welding programs must teach the fundamentals of welding, but once a student has the fundamentals, what area of welding are you as the instructor going to have the student focus upon? This is where your experience comes in. If you are a fabricator, then your welding program should focus on fabrication. If your experience is ship building, then you program should lean heavily toward maritime welding. Use your experience to focus the welding program but also make sure you are teaching your students skills they can use to get a job. If there are no fabrication jobs in your area, but there are construction jobs, you should take the initiative to learn construction welding techniques and teach those techniques to the students so that they can more easily obtain employment in the area where there is demand for welders. The best way to know what area has the most demand for welders is by having an active advisory committee. A discussion on advisory committees comes later.

\

Chapter 2

Recruiting

Your best recruiting tool is a successful student. A successful student will go back home after working and have a pocket full of money. They will hang out with all their friends showing off the money that they have made. Their friends will ask how they can make that kind of money, and that is when your student will tell them all about welding and about your program and you become a hero. Do your best to give every student the opportunity to be successful. Not all of them will make it, but they all need equal opportunity.

Besides successful students, the next best thing to recruit good students is to go to the high schools and talk to teachers and students yourself. I know not everyone is comfortable speaking in front of people, but this is something you as the instructor will need to do. My college has several people hired as recruiters and they do a good job recruiting for other programs, but only a welder can truly talk about welding. I know the way to "push the buttons" of the high school students that will make good welders. You have to sell welding. It is something you will have to develop. I know instructors who do not recruit at the local high schools. These instructors say is not part of their job, and that that is the job of the recruiters. Maybe so, but their welding programs are suffering. You get out what you put in. If you rely on someone else to recruit for you, you will not have strong numbers. But if you get out there and go to the local high schools and talk welding up, you should have strong student numbers.

When I talk to high school students, I tell them about how welding builds our world and how our way of life is dependent on welding. Then I show them pay stubs of past graduates and that gets their attention. Because as you know, money talks!! If you have some successful students, get a copy of some of their pay stubs and show them off. If possible, take a successful student who's graduated from your program to the local schools with you. This gives the high school students someone they can relate to a little bit better than you. Recruiting is one of those things that academic instructors don't necessarily have to do, but as a technical instructor you will need to do so to have a successful program.

Another way I recruit students is by offering training outside of my regular welding classes. I give weld camps to the local boy scout troops so that they can get their welding merit badge. These scouts are usually in junior high and just starting to find out what interests them for job possibilities. Hosting a camp for boy scouts is a good way to get them excited about welding and plant the idea about welding as a career that might bring them back when they graduate high school. Plus, it lets kids from other communities that you might not visit know about your program.

I also host a summer welding camp for high school girls. It is usually 3 days long and I teach the girls MIG welding. On the last day, I help the girls build a small project, like a dragonfly statue. This girls camp has been very successful in letting these high school girls know that there are other career options besides just going to college to be a teacher or nurse. I have a couple of female students that have graduated and have become successful in the welding industry help me during the girl's camp. These returning female students give the girl campers someone that they can relate to and say, "If she can do it, so can I."

I also started a weekend hobby welding class. This is aimed at older people from the community that want to learn to weld so that they can do projects in their home workshops. I don't get many direct students from these classes but the ones that participate in the hobby classes might have a child or grandchild that could become a student. The weekend hobby classes are another way of getting the word out about the welding program and to showcase the college.

Chapter 3

Curriculum and Classroom Management

Curriculum

There are numerous choices of welding curriculums. There is the Hobart Institute of Welding Technology, American Welding Society S.E.N.S.E., and the National Center of Construction Education and Research (NCCER), to name just a few. Plus, there are several traditional text books, like *Modern Welding*, from which to choose. You need to find the book or curriculum that you understand and that you are most comfortable teaching.

I personally like the NCCER welding curriculum. To me the NCCER curriculum has several advantages over the other curricula. First, the NCCER curriculum has separated each welding process into its own level and each level has a separate book. This is an advantage because your students do not have to buy a big bulky, expensive book at the beginning. The expense of the books can be spread throughout the program because they only need the book for the process they are currently studying.

Each level, or book, is divided into chapters, or in NCCER terms, modules. Each module is stand alone, which means you can teach the modules in any order you wish. There is no pre-determined order that you have to follow. Some of the chapters make sense to teach before others. For example, it makes sense to teach SMAW Equipment and Filler Metals before SMAW Beads and Fillet Welds, but it is your choice. It is this flexibility of the NCCER curriculum that I really like. I can teach the modules in the order that matches the way I have laid out the welding program.

Another thing I like about the NCCER curriculum is that it can be used to get your students industry recognized credentialing that meets the Perkins Grant requirements. To do this, your program will need to be a NCCER Accredited Training and Educational Facility. To get this accreditation, your program will need a training sponsor, and you as an instructor will need to be trained as a NCCER instructor, and your shop will need to meet a few design requirements. You can find more detailed information about becoming an ATEF on the NCCER website, www.nccer.org. NCCER curriculum is nationally recognized and meets most federal and state requirements for funding programs.

The way in which I have the welding program laid out is largely dictated by the state. The state I currently teach in has two certificates in welding: Welding Technology and Welding Technology-Advanced. The state decided what welding processes are to be taught in each certificate, but the instructors are allowed a great deal of flexibility within each certificate of how the welding program could be set up.

I teach stick welding in the first semester, followed by MIG, Flux Core, and TIG plate in the second semester to complete the Welding Technology certificate. The Welding Technology-Advanced Certificate is two more semesters of pipe welding. I teach SMAW pipe followed by GTAW carbon pipe and finish up with stainless steel pipe. I start with stick welding because there not a lot of manufacturing or fabrication welding jobs in the local area. If a student learns stick welding and for some reason cannot finish the welding program, they should be able to get a welding job as a structural welder for a construction company. At past schools, I taught MIG welding first because there were several metal manufacturing plants in the area and a student that knew how to MIG weld could find work locally. Work within your state's framework to set up your welding program to meet the needs of your local employers. The welding program might already be set up when you get hired, but it is not written in stone, so tweak it as much as you need to make it fit your area.

The First Day of Class

The first day of class is an exciting day. The new students are excited because they are starting a journey toward a new career. I am excited because of the potential the new students have. You can feel the energy in the room.

The first day of class in my program is not the typical first day for an academic student. A lot of college professors cover the course syllabus then send students home. It is traditionally a short day. Not in my class! I keep students the whole day.

I use the first day to set the tone for the semester and for the program. I do this with my opening statement. In that opening statement, I emphasize that the students are adults and I will treat them like adults. I am there to guide them through the weld training but I am not a life coach. I tell them that all of their decisions going forward have long reaching effects and that the students should rely on their faith and their family to guide them.

I say this to my students to let them know this is not your typical welding program. The little speech I give lets my students know that I will not baby them. Of course, I will help them where I can; however, I am their welding instructor first and foremost. These first statements get the students into a serious mind set for the program.

The students who usually have issues with the tone I set for the program are students straight out of high school. These students expect my program to be the same atmosphere as high school. Well, it is not. My students are 18 years old or older, and therefore adults. I treat them like adults. I do this by giving them information, making sure they understand this information, then I hold them accountable for this information. A lot of the students that have just graduated from high school are not used to being treated like adults. My welding program helps them to start thinking as an adult.

Now that the tone is set, I do the typical college first day things. I hand out and go over the course syllabus, the lecture schedule, the weld test schedule, and most importantly, the Conduct and Dress Code. The Conduct and Dress Code are the safety guidelines for the shop.
I hand the conduct sheet to every student, every semester. I read every line of the Conduct and Dress Code to the students and make sure they understand what the safety guidelines are. The second page of this document is a signature page. The students print their name, they date it, and they sign the sheet acknowledging that they understand the safety guidelines to the shop and agree to follow them.

After the rules have been established, and we have gone over the syllabus, I do a safety presentation. It consists of a short but thorough PowerPoint® and a written test. A student must make a 90%, or higher, on the safety test to be allowed into the weld shop. If the student doesn't make a 90% or higher, I go over the safety material in a one-on-one session with the student to make sure that they understand all the safety rules for the welding shop.

After the safety test, I go over the equipment the students will be using in the shop. I show them how to use an angle grinder, how to set up the welding equipment, and how to weld. I do this because, afterwards, we go to the shop and weld. Yes, I have my students welding on the first day of class. This is shocking to most of my new students. They think we will sit in the classroom for a day or two talking about safety and watching videos on welding before we go into the shop to weld. They are wrong! We weld the first day because the only way to learn to weld is to weld.

The Classroom

The classroom is the second most important area in a welding program. This is where the students will be learning the technical side of welding. The classroom should be a separate room from the shop. It is very hard to conduct a lesson while trying to shout over grinding and banging of metal in the background.

The classroom should be well lit and climate controlled. In today's society, that is usually not a problem. The classroom should also have an overhead projector set up for computer connection. This will be used for any Power Point presentations or for showing videos as part of a chapter lecture. I find that tables and chairs are better than desks. This is because in our society people are getting bigger and a desk can be very uncomfortable for someone that is of a larger size. If you have tables and chairs, this is not an issue. I like 6-foot-long tables with 2 chairs per table. This gives enough room for students at the table but does not take up much more room than 2 desks set side by side. I have set the tables up in a U-shape configuration, and also in traditional rows. The configuration you set the tables in is up to you, but you have to make sure the tables are set up in a way where the students can see you during presentations, and also be able to see the overhead screen. Also, the classroom configuration should allow you to move about the room easily. If you, or the students, have to struggle to get around the tables and chairs, it is not a good set up and you should make adjustments.

Another item I like to have in my classroom is a small cabinet to hold visual aids for lectures. I have several visual aids I use, such as a cut away oxy/fuel torch, a cut away gas regulator, a pipe backing ring, and a dye penetrate kit, among others. Having these in a cabinet in the classroom makes it easy to find the visual aid I need for a lecture.

The classroom can get cluttered and junky very quickly. I have seen welding programs where the instructor's desk has been full of junk, and actually hazardous. The desk had no real purpose in the room but to hold junk. I know there are a lot of items you will want to show your students, but be careful not to leave too many things lying around. I have seen many classrooms that look like junk yards. Don't let your classroom look like a junk yard. Have only the items you need for teaching the class.

Classroom Management

I base a lot of my classroom management on what my welding instructor did and didn't do. My welding instructor was my father, Frank Smith. He was a great welding instructor that helped numerous people change their lives with welding, but he hated the classroom and it showed. He did his best, but the classroom days were so long. Frank would give a lecture by standing at a podium and talking for 2 hours. It would put just about everyone to sleep.

Why even give a lecture? I believe technical instructors should give lectures to their students when introducing new ideas and concepts from the textbook. A lot of technical instructors have their students read the textbook on their own, outside of the classroom time, without any guidance. I find this method of teaching the book work of a program problematic. It is problematic to me because a new technical idea might need further explanation than just what the book gives. The role of an instructor is to explain complex technical ideas and concepts in simpler terms. Terms that a student can understand so that the student can put the ideas and concepts into practice.

When I became an instructor, I asked myself, "How can I make the lectures better?" The answer was interesting PowerPoint® presentations and relevant videos. I have created a PowerPoint® presentation for every chapter I teach, and I have inserted videos into the PowerPoint® presentations where suitable. This does several things to help maximize the classroom time and improve the lectures.

By using a PowerPoint® presentation for each lecture, it helps me deliver the same information to each group of students. At the beginning of my teaching career, I found myself skipping information in lectures because I thought I had already shared that information with the group of students I was lecturing. The PowerPoint® presentations helped me to deliver the same information year after year to various student groups.

In the PowerPoint® presentations, I have highlighted sentences that have important safety information or main points that may become test questions. I have my students follow in their books, and I have them highlight these important sentences. This helps keep their attention during the lecture, plus it makes them read the information as they highlight. This allows them to receive the information in two ways: visually from reading and highlighting them, and the other, audibly from my lecture. This form of lecture with PowerPoint® presentations and with pointing out highlightable materials has really helped my students to retain book knowledge associated with the trade. I also use the review questions in the NCCER modules to help my students retain valuable information.

I use review questions as a pre-lecture study guide. I require my students to do the chapter review questions before lectures. I check to make sure they have completed the questions, and then we go over the review questions before the lecture. This way I know the students have at least looked at the chapter and are familiar with the content. Making this a required step, the students are more engaged in the lectures, and their grades on their chapter tests have improved.

I am very specific about the answer sheets for these review questions. On the students' review question answer sheets, I require their name, date, chapter, and the chapter title in specific places on their paper. The student's name goes in the top right-hand corner, and the date of the assignment goes below their name, followed by the chapter number. The title of the chapter has to be written on the top line of the paper. The answers for the review questions are multiple choice, and I will not accept the homework if the student just writes the letter answer. They must write the letter answer and then write out the answer choice, for example: 1) A – work angle.

If the student completes the homework paper in this manner, they get a grade of 100%. If they do not put the name, date, chapter number, or chapter name in the correct spot, they get a grade of 75%. If they do not write out the answers, I do not accept the homework paper and they get a 0 as the grade for that assignment. I do not grade whether the students got the correct answers on the homework, but I grade whether they did the assignment and followed directions. That is what I am trying to teach my students with the homework papers: follow directions and pay attention to details. The homework papers are a small way of teaching these lessons over and over throughout the welding program. Learning to follow instructions and paying attention to details are lessons that are important in almost every area of life.

I have talked about homework and giving a lecture using PowerPoint® presentations, so what, you may ask, is my schedule for giving these lectures? It depends on the semester, but I always give a lecture or chapter test on either Tuesday or Thursday. I stay away from requiring any work on Mondays. I have found that Mondays are not good days for students. Most of my students work on weekends and do not have a lot of free time on weekends.

I like giving lectures on a Thursday and having the chapter tests on the following Tuesday. I have found that this gives students time to do the homework before the lecture and time to study for the tests. I also like this schedule because it helps me focus the lectures on one subject at a time. An instructor might have to give more than one lecture a week, depending on the curriculum and how much time is needed to cover the required material.

Remember one important thing when giving a lecture: the brain can only absorb what the rear end can withstand. Make sure to give the students breaks to stand up, and to move around, and to go to the restroom. I usually give a break every 30 minutes, and I limit my lectures to two hours, max. If the material of the lecture requires more time, I break the material into two different lectures. No welding student I have every taught liked sitting in the classroom too long, and I don't like being in the classroom talking for too long. I know some welding schools have lectures all day long, for one day a week. I think this is a bad idea. Have shorter sessions, more times per week.

I have a lecture schedule and chapter schedule laid out before each semester, and I give a copy to the students on the first day of class. This way they know what homework is due when and when the chapter tests will be conducted. My students do not have the excuse of "I didn't know the lecture was today." I strongly adhere to the lecture schedules and to the test schedules. I don't change these schedules unless the circumstances are out of my control, and I let my students know as soon as I can that there is a change to the schedule. These schedules help keep everyone on the same page and gets the students into a routine for having homework assignments done, and for studying for tests. I also set a schedule for weld tests throughout the semester.

Another thing I do differently than most other technical program instructors is calling roll every morning and again after lunch. I know of several instructors that let students sign in and out. I don't like that system because it is too easy for a student to sign their friend in and/or out. I like to call roll and look the students in the eyes when I say their name. That way I know for sure who is present and who is absent. I do the same thing after lunch to see if anybody has left early for the day.

The reason I do two (2) roll calls is because my program has a very strict attendance policy. If a student misses more that 10% of their scheduled class times, they fail that class. Two (2) early outs counts as an absence. Also, I do not believe in tardies. If a student comes in late to class, they are sent home and counted absent for that day and that counts against the 10%. If they cannot be on time, they cannot come into the classroom. The students expect me to be on time and ready to teach class, so I expect them to be on time and ready to learn. It is a hard stance but being at work on time is important for keeping a job. This is another way I teach the soft skills to my students, so that they will be successful in a welding career.

Chapter 4

Toolroom Management

The tool room in my shop is impressive. It is impressive not because it is large or has exotic tools in it. The toolroom is impressive because it is very neat and orderly. I have a place for everything and everything is in its place. I have a grinder and a clear face shield for each weld booth. Yes, I have 30 grinders and 30 face shields in my shop.

Figure 1: Tool Room

Figure 2: Tool Room, view of hand tool wall & TIG rigs

Figure 3: Angle Grinders

Figure 4: Rod oven and grinding discs

I labeled each grinder and face shield with the booth number to which they are assigned. I assign each student a weld booth, grinder, and face shield at the beginning of each semester. The student is responsible for this grinder and face shield during the semester. If the grinders are damaged due to misuse or abuse, the student is financially responsible for replacing them. If they break it, they replace it!

I have the grinders hanging on the wall. I mounted a strip of 1/8" bent plate to the wall and hang the grinders on the strip by their guards. The face shields are hung on hooks on the wall. I can take a quick look and see if a grinder or face shield is missing.

The small amount of hand tools that I keep in the tool room are hung on the wall as well. I have a few adjustable wrenches, levels, open-box end wrench sets, and a couple of hammers. These tools are outlined or shadow boxed. This makes it easy to see at a glance if any of the tools are missing.

For small tools and welding parts that cannot hang on the wall, I have a small cabinet in the tool room. In this cabinet, there are small labeled bins to hold the various parts. It is easy for these bins to get disorganized and junky, so I have a student regularly go through these bins to keep them straight.

Toolroom Attendant and Strawboss

One of the reasons my tool room stays neat and orderly is that I use a tool room attendant. If I allowed 30 students to bum rush the tool room each morning to get tools, the tool room would be a disaster, so I use a tool room attendant. The tool room attendant is a student that I assign to be in charge of the tool room for the week. Each morning the tool room attendant hands out the tools to the other students, after they sign the tools out, and every afternoon the tool room attendant receives the tools from the other students. This keeps the traffic down in the tool room during start up and shut down of each day. The tool room attendant does not stay in the tool room all day. The scheduled student tends the tool room for the first 30 minutes of the day and the last 20 minutes of the day. If you do not use a tool room attendant, I strongly suggest you implement this. A tool room attendant is very helpful.

Another program I use, to help keep the shop orderly and teach leadership skills to my students, is the strawboss. The strawboss is the lead student for the week. The main duties of the strawboss is to help the tool room attendant in the morning, handing out tools and receiving tools in the afternoon. The strawboss is also in charge of the afternoon clean up.

At the end of class time, I do not clean up anything. The students do the cleanup. Each student is responsible for cleaning their booth, and then they are to help clean the common areas of the shop, like the grinding booths. The strawboss is tasked with making sure that each student does his or her part in the cleanup. When the strawboss tells me everything is good, I do a walk-through inspection. If I find something that is not up to my standards, I have the strawboss direct a student to correct the discrepancy. This way the students learn leadership and how to direct people. Each student gets to be the strawboss each semester. This ensures that if one student gets "power hungry" and abuses the strawboss position, it will come back to them the next week when a different student is the strawboss.

I also put the strawboss in charge of small tasks that need to be done around the shop, such as cutting metal for weld practice. I will inform the strawboss of what the task is and give him or her the details of the task, then the strawboss is to assign students to complete the task. I do not expect the strawboss to complete every task. The strawboss is to assign the tasks, then supervise the completion of the tasks. Of course, I am nearby supervising the whole operation to make sure it is done safely.

I have found that using students as strawbosses or tool room attendants has really helped them to gain confidence, develop leadership skills, and these responsibilities make the students better team players because they understand what is involved in supervising a team.

Chapter 5

Setting up the Weld Shop

The welding shop or lab is where welding students will spend most of their time learning, so the space in the shop should be utilized as efficiently as possible. Most curricula, such as NCCER and AWS SENSE, have some basic guidelines on the amount of space a shop should have per student. There are OSHA, state, and sometimes local guidelines on the amount of air changes and space requirements in a weld training facility, so be mindful of these guidelines when setting up a new shop or making changes to an existing facility.

The welding shop layout should consider optimum use of the space. In welding shops I have designed, I did my best to have a good work flow to the shop. I did this by asking a few questions:

Where is the metal stored?

How and where are the students going to cut the metal?

What is the most direct path from the metal storage area to the saw and/or shear?

Where is the best spot for the grinding booths?

Where is the best area for torch cutting?

How many weld booths can fit and it not be over-crowded?

Where is the best location for the welding machines?

I used these questions to come up with a common-sense flow for the students from the metal storage area to the welding booth. I look for the most direct path for this flow and place the shop equipment, such as the band saw, the metal shear, and cutting torches, in such a way as to facilitate that flow.

Most welding shops have several large tables in the middle of the shop and smaller tables along the walls of the shop. I hate tables! Unless a table has a specific purpose, all it does is collect junk! I have only one table in my shop and it was built with a specific purpose. It is for the bench grinders. That is the only table I have, and I still have to be vigilant to keep it clean. Horizontal surfaces collect stuff. Limit the number of tables in your shop. The fewer horizontal surfaces, the easier it will be to keep your shop clean. If you must have a table, make sure the students clean it off every day. If you let things start to pile up, it will get junky quickly and become hard to keep clean.

The most important part of a welding shop is the weld booths. The booths are where most of the learning takes place. So, the weld booths should be large enough so that the student is not cramped but not so large that the booth takes up too much floor space. The size of the weld booths will also determine the number of booths in the shop and therefore, the number of students you will have in the shop. In weld training facilities I have set up or redesigned, I built the weld booths 5 feet wide, 5 feet deep and 7 feet tall. The walls of the weld booths are 5 feet, leaving a 2-foot space at the bottom to allow for air flow. The frames for the weld booths are made from 1-1/2" square tubing and the walls are 16-gauge sheet metal. I use strip weld curtains on the weld booths. I like the strip curtains because they always stay closed. I have used weld curtains that slide from the side, but the students hardly ever closed the curtains, and this is a safety concern. I design the weld booths with a weld stand. I do not use tables in the weld booths. A table takes up too much room and it collects junk. The weld stand has a main pole of 2-inch pipe that is 6ft.5in. tall on a 12in. x 12in. base plate of 3/8in. thickness with 5/8in. holes in the corners for an anchor bolt. I have an arm with a 2 1/2in. pipe sleeve that has a tightening bolt attached to it. This sleeve slides up and down the pole. The arm that comes off the sleeve is 2in. square tubing. On the arm is a "table" made up of a square tubing sleeve with a tightening bolt welded to a 3/8in. thick x 8in. x 10in. plate. This is the table to which the students tack weld their practice pieces. This set up is different than most weld stands because most weld stands have 2 in. pipe for the arm. I have square tubing because the table cannot slip on the square tubing.

In one shop where I taught, the weld stand arms were pipe. I had one student nearly lose his front teeth because of these pipe arms. He was practicing on an overhead 1in. v-groove plate. He tightened the securing bolt on his arm as much as he could, but because of weld spatter it was not enough, and his weld practice piece rotated and fell into his face. After that day, I refitted the weld stand arms with square tubing and have not had a problem like that since.

I mount the weld stands in the left back corner of the weld booth with the main pole 10 inches from the walls. I find this best utilizes the space in the weld booth. These stands work well for right and left-handed students.

Figure 5: Welding booth exterior

Figure 6: Weld stand with table

I have a pipe stand that slides on the square arm. This pipe stand has 3 position holes that hold pipe in 2G, 6G, and 5G positions. The pipe stand has a purge hole in it that is large enough for the end of a purge hose to slip into. We use this when purging bi-metal pipe and stainless-steel pipe for welding. Having a multiple position pipe stand that slides on the square tube arm saves a lot of space in the booth. The weld stands don't have a lot of arms sticking out of them that get in the way of the students. We have a storage peg welded on the back wall of the booth behind the weld stand for storing the pipe stand. This keeps the pipe stand out of the way but ready when the student needs it for practicing. I also have a small triangular shelf in the right back corner of the booth about waist high. This shelf is used to hold small items. I use expanded metal for the shelf so that it will not collect dust or junk. This shelf is 18in. across the front and is just large enough to hold a few hand tools, such as side cutters or an adjustable wrench. It helps keep these items off the floor and within easy reach for the students. I have 110-volt power outlets in each weld booth. These outlets are for the use of grinders in the booths when necessary. Because the students have grinders in the booths, I built grinder holders in the booths. The grinder holders are a piece of 1/8-inch sheet metal bent at a 90-degree angle with 2-inch sides, and 6 inches long. This is welded to the side of the booth at 36 inches from the bottom of the booth wall. The grinder is hung up by its guard on the bent plate. I find this does no damage to the grinder and hangs it neatly out of the way. Above the grinder holder is a face shield hook. I have a grinder and face shield for each booth and require my students to use a face shield whenever they use a grinder or any tool that creates a spark. These holders and hooks help keep the weld booths neat and safe.

Figure 7: Angle grinder and face shield in weld booth

Figure 8: Grinding and oxy-fuel cutting area

Figure 9: Weld stand with pipe stand

Speaking of grinding, now would be a good time tell you about my grinding booths. I do have grinding booths set up in an area outside the weld shop. Not all shops have the space for a set up like this, but you need grinding booths. By grinding booths, I don't mean a table with a vise on it. I think that is one of the worst set ups ever. Why? Because the tables are usually built with the tops at waist high and then a vise is put on it. This puts the metal a student is grinding on at almost chest high and that is very uncomfortable and dangerous. It is dangerous because it becomes difficult to control a grinder having to hold it at chest height. Also, the tables are usually in the middle of the shop and don't have any type of curtain around them to contain the sparks.

Figure 10: Vise on a tripod mount

Figure 11: Vise close-up & Vise in a grinding booth

My grinding booths are individual booths that are 4 ft.6 in. square and 7-foot-tall. The walls are 4 foot. This allows a little more room at the bottom for air flow in the grind booths. I have strip curtains on the grind booths just like the weld booths. These curtains really help contain the sparks.

I put the top of the vise in my grind booths at 36 inches, just about belt buckle height. At this height, the students are able to control the grinders better and it is a more comfortable working height. I have mounted vises on a 3-leg stand and have mounted them on a single leg stand anchored to the concrete. The three-legged stand is stable and is able to be moved around for clean-up. The single leg stand is permanently anchored in the weld booth to provide a solid base for the vise. This stand has a 2in. piece of pipe with a 3/8in. plate welded to both ends. One end has holes for 3/8in. anchor bolts to anchor the stand to the concrete. The plate, on the other end, is used to mount the vise. The height of the vise is 36in. on the single leg stand. Make sure the stands for the vises are solid and safe for students to work.

The grind booths also have a double 110-volt power outlet installed in them. This way a student can use an angle grinder and an end grinder in the booth at the same time if needed. I have 2 grinder hangers in the grind booths to help keep the grinder off the ground and the booths neat. The weld booths and the grind booths are both painted a light tan color. No, I do not paint my weld booths black! They do not have to be a dark color. Just paint them with a flat paint. The flat paint will not reflect the ultra violet rays that burn your eyes. Having the booths painted a light tan color will make them brighter and makes the shop look brighter and neater.

Each of my welding booths and grinding booths have a 4-foot light over them. These really help the students to be able to see while they are working. I have worked in shops that did not have a light over the booths and these lights make a huge difference. I recommend working with your maintenance crew to have lights installed over your weld booths and grind booths if you do not have them.

Now that I have given you an idea of how I layout my welding shop, I'm going to discuss welding machines and their location in the shop.

I use multi-process inverter welding machines in my shop. The reason I like these machines is that they can weld the four main welding processes, shielded metal arc welding, gas metal arc welding, flux core arc welding, and gas tungsten arc welding. I have a multi-process machine at each booth so that I can teach each process at each booth. I don't like having certain weld booths for certain welding processes. This limits the number of students you can have learning that process. I know one instructor that got in a jam because he had more students in the class for a welding process than he had booths. He was scrambling to figure out what to do with the "extra" students. It was not a good situation for the instructor or the students.

With each multi-process welding machine, I also have a wire feeder. Each of the booths in my shop can run any of the welding processes I teach. Having this type of machine and a wire feeder for each booth is not cheap, but it makes your shop more versatile. I believe the flexibly that this machine and feeder set up allows is worth the cost.

Where do I keep these welding machines in my shop layout? Good question. The welding machine should be close to the student so they can make adjustments but out of the way so as not to be a trip hazard or blocking a walk way.

Most shops have the weld booths all side by side sharing a wall. This design saves on material and makes the shop look nice and neat, until you add in the welding machines. Shops with this weld booth set up usually put the welding machines in front of the weld booths. This keeps the machines close but it blocks access to the weld booths and the weld cables become tripping hazards in the walk ways. Another option I see a lot is putting the welding machines in the booths with the students. This set up takes up a lot of room in the weld booth. I tried this set up for a little bit, but the students and myself hated it. So, I came up with what I think is the best set up. I keep the welding machines between the weld booths. Let me explain.

I grouped the booths into sets of 4's. 2 booths side by side and back to back. Then I separated the groups of 4 by a 36 inch "alley way". This alley way is where I have the welding machines. The welding machines are beside the booths so the students have easy access to them, but the machines and cables are out of the walk way and do not create a tripping hazard. This set up also helps give the shop a neat and orderly look.

The current weld shop I teach in is a 50-foot x 100-foot pre-engineered metal building with a 14-foot awning, and 4 rollup doors. The building is 16-foot at the eves. There are three offices at the front of the shop going across the

50-foot width. The bandsaw and metal shear are at the end of the shop opposite the offices. The tool room and two restrooms are part of a 14-foot awning that was enclosed about a year after the welding program started. I have 30 weld booths in the shop and each one is numbered. I set the weld booths up running long ways down the shop. From the front of the shop you can see down the walkways to the back of the shop. This makes the shop seem open and spacious.

I have a 5-foot walk way between the rows of weld booths and from the shop walls to the booths. 5-foot is enough room for 2 adults to comfortably walk past each other. The rows of weld booths start about 12 feet from my office wall and they stop 20 feet from the back-shop wall. This 20-foot area is where I have my band saw and metal shear. I made sure that there was a wide, clear walk-way from the metal storage rack to the band saw and shear area.

Figure 12: Welding Shop

Figure 13: Welding Shop

Figure 14: Welding Shop

Figure 15: Welding Shop

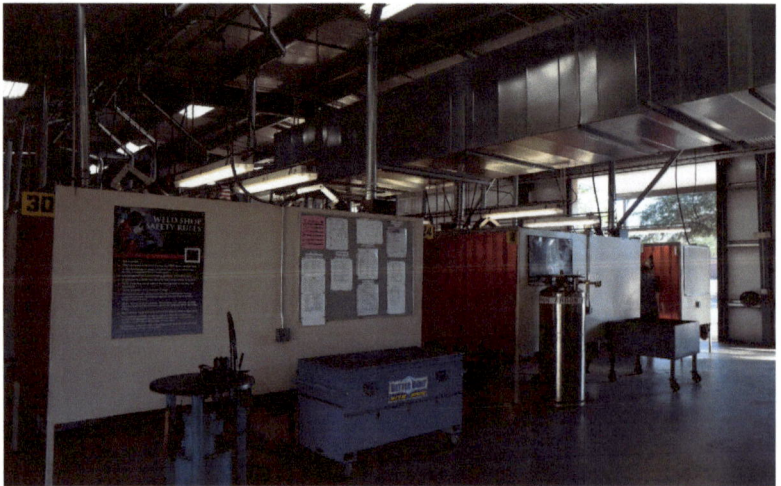

Figure 16: Welding Shop

In 2017, a 20' x 50' area was added to the end of the weld shop. This area was covered and the front enclosed with a roll up door. The other 2 sides were left open for air circulation. I used this area to add more grinding booths and to have a larger flame cutting area.

I do not have a large fabrication area in the center of my shop. This is because I do not teach fabrication. My shop is set up to make optimum use of the space I have for the purpose of teaching pipe welding. You should set your shop up to teach your area of concentration of welding. If you are planning on having projects and teaching fabrication, then have a fabrication area set up, but don't have a fabrication area for no reason. Make sure your weld shop is set up for your style of teaching.

Chapter 6

Weld Tests

When I was in welding school, my teacher, my father, did a few things that really bugged me as a student. One was that there was not a schedule for weld practices in the shop. The other was there was not a set criteria for grading a weld test.

In my father's program, when a student got proficient at a weld practice, say for example, 7018 horizontal tee fillet welds, my father would say, "Alright, the next weld will be your test." There was no schedule or set time for when the practice of one particular weld had to be completed. This allowed some students to practice on one weld for several weeks and they would get behind on their lab exercises for that semester. So, at the end of the semester that student would be turning in a bunch of weld "tests" just so they could get some grade for doing the work.

When I started teaching, I made up a weld test schedule so that my students would know exactly how much time they would have to practice a weld and when the weld test was going to be held. I have set up my current weld program for 5 days a week, 7 hours a day, for a total of 35 hours a week. I hold weld tests on the last day of the training week. At my current school, it is Friday. This schedule helps students to improve time management. If the students stand around and talks all week, they lose valuable weld practice time and their weld test grade reflects this. But if a student shows me that they are proficient at the weld for that week, I allow them to move ahead and practice another weld.

I know everyone learns at a different rate and people have told me that holding to a weld test schedule handicaps the people that learn at a slower rate. This might be true, but every job I have been on has a schedule and a welder is paid to meet that schedule. If a person cannot meet the weld test schedule, they probably will not be able to meet the job schedule. I use the weld test schedule to get my students into the mindset that there is a schedule you will have to meet. Just letting students test when they are ready, in my opinion, is not preparing them for the job environment they will enter.

The weld test schedule should be set up to cover all the required material of that semester but be at a pace that the average student can maintain. You will always have the students that catch on quickly and get ahead and there will always be the ones that can't keep up. Once again, the schedule should be for the average student. You, as the instructor, have to realize that not everyone is going to make it as a welder, and you will lose some of your students. The administration will not want to hear this but it is a fact. Not everyone can be a welder and having the weld test on a regular schedule will help weed out those students that cannot make it.

Now that you have established a weld test schedule, how are your students going to practice? They practice like it is the test. You have the students use the same material for practice as they would use for the test. The materials I use are 1/4-inch plate, 3/8-inch plate, 1-inch plate, 6-inch pipe schedule 40 and 80, and 2-inch pipe schedule 160. For stainless, I have 2-inch schedule 40 and schedule 10 pipe.

For practice welding on plate, I have my students use 7018 - 1/8-inch rods on 3/8-inch plate. The 7018 tee joint coupons are 3 inches wide and 12 inches long. I make the coupons 12 inches long so the students have to do a restart in the weld. I know some instructors that use 6-inch long coupons, but their students are not very good at restarts. Practicing restarts on plate, makes restarts on pipe much easier. I test my students in three positions on plate using 7018 rods, 2F, 3F, and 4F.

With 6010 rods, I make my students use 1/8-inch rods on 1/4-inch plate and the tee joint coupons are 2 inches by 6 inches. I use 6-inch coupons for 6010 because with the whip-and-pause technique, every puddle is like a restart. I test my students on 6010 rod in the same three (3) positions that I test them on with 7018 rod, 2F, 3F, and 4F.

For V-groove welds, I use 3/8-inch plate and 1-inch plate. I follow the AWS D1.1 guidelines for setup of the coupons for these practices and tests. I use 1/4-inch x 2-inch flat bar as the backing strip for these welds. Flat bar is very convenient for this.

For stick pipe, I have my students practice and test on 6-inch schedule 40 pipe. This schedule pipe is a little thin for stick but it makes my students work harder to be good at it. Plus, most stick pipe is chilled water line and it is schedule 40 pipe.

I use the 6-inch schedule 80 pipe for TIG/Stick combo pipe practices and test. This thicker pipe gives my students more hood time on pipe. Schedule 80 gives them more pipe to fill up. I make them do pipe test TIG all the way out in the 2G, 5G and 6G pipe positions. They also have to do a combo pipe test in all 3 positions. I also require my pipe students to do a test on stainless schedule 40 in the 2G, 5G and 6G positions and a stainless schedule 10 in the 6G position.

Once the weld tests are scheduled, and the students have practiced, how do you grade a weld test? The way my father graded weld tests always bugged me and it is the manner in which most welding instructors grade weld tests. They look at the weld and decide on a grade. This manner of grading is very subjective and is usually done in front of the student so the instructor knows whose weld test they are grading. I conduct my weld tests in a different manner, and I grade my students' weld tests in a non-subjective manner.

How do I conduct my weld tests? I conduct my weld tests like certification tests for a welding job in a test shop. I give the weld tests on a set day like I mentioned earlier. I give the weld tests at set times, usually after morning break, so 9:45am on Fridays. Everyone in a class takes the same weld test at the same time. Even if students in the class are practicing ahead, they "drop back" and take the weld test with the rest of their class.

I have the weld test pieces cut the day before the tests and I hand them out to the students just like an inspector would do in a test shop. I have the students mark their weld test pieces with their welder I.D. number. I have the students use the last 4 digits of their student I.D. number as their welder I.D. This way I do not know whose test I am grading and the grade will be as non-subjective as possible.

The students tack their weld test pieces together and tack them into position in their weld booths. I then go around and inspect that the fit up on the test pieces is correct and that the test pieces are in the correct position for the weld test that the students are taking. This is the first of three hold points in the testing process. If something is not right, I have the student correct it, but this cuts into this student's test time. Yes, I give them a time limit on their weld tests. Like I said earlier, I treat their weld tests just like a weld test for a job in a test shop, so there is a time limit.

After the student puts the first welds on each side of a fillet weld, I check it. This is just like checking the root weld on a pipe test. I never stop a student from completing the weld test at this hold point, but it gets the student used to having to stop and get the inspector to check the weld.

The last hold point is the completed weld. I check the weld when the student says it is completed. The student is not supposed to move the weld coupon during the test or take it down until after I have done the final check. If the student moves the weld coupon during the test, or takes it down before the final check, they receive a grade of 65, which is an F in our grading scale.

This method of conducting a weld test is as close to a job certification test as I can get it. By doing this on a weekly basis, my students learn to deal with test jitters so that the jitters will not affect their welding on a test for a job. This method has helped numerous students get over their test anxieties.

I usually grade the weld tests the following Monday. This gives the weld tests plenty of time to cool off so I can handle them, plus it allows time for me to forget whose weld looked like what. I do not want to know whose weld test I am grading so the grade will be as impartial as possible. The only identifying mark on the weld test is the student's I.D. number and I make a point of not learning those.

I grade the weld tests a lot differently than how my dad graded my weld test back in weld school. I would bring him my weld test, he would look at it and come up with a grade. Not really having a set standard of what was an A, B, or a C for a weld test. This would irritate me because I thought my welds that got a B, looked a lot better than some of the guys' welds that received an A. I would ask my dad why I received a B, and he would say, "Your weld looked like a B to me and that is good enough. Now go practice more." So, when I started teaching welding, I wanted to have a set standard for grading weld tests.

What I came up with is a grading rubric that looks at 10 different aspects of a fillet weld. These 10 aspects are based off the NCCER performance evaluation sheet and the AWS D1.1 code book for structural welds. Each aspect is a line item on the weld grade worksheet. Each line item is worth 6 points.

The 10 visual aspects I look at on fillet welds:

1) Uniform rippled appearance on the bead face
2) Craters and restarts filled to the full cross section of the weld
3) Uniform weld size within 1/16 of an inch.
4) Acceptable weld profile in accordance with AWS D1.1 code.
5) Smooth transition with compete fusion at the toe of the weld
6) Porosity
7) Undercut
8) Cold Lap
9) Strick marks
10) Visual appearance

Let's say for example, we are grading a 7018 horizontal fillet weld. The test is a single bead weld on one side of the joint and a 3-bead weld on the other side of the joint. I look at both welds together, and grade both sides as one weld. Let's say the weld has a section of undercut, a strike mark and cold lap on the 3-bead side. This weld test would get a grade of 82. Start at 100 and subtract 6 points for each discontinuity of the weld, so 3 discontinuities x 6 points each = 18 points, so I subtract 18 points from 100 = 82.

In this grading system, it does not matter if you have one strike mark or 20 strike marks, 6 points is deducted from the grade for strike marks. The same goes for undercut or any of the other visual discontinuities I see. If the weld has a little or a lot, it carries the same amount of points. Using this system, I can explain to the student what I counted off for and justify their grade. There is no arguing over a grade when the criteria for the grade is spelled out and consistently followed. Me and my students have found this system helps them know what they did wrong on the weld test and it helps them learn to inspect their welds. This grading system has been a real help in improving my teaching and keeping the grading consistent over the years.

The testing process is very similar for a V-groove weld test on plate and pipe. I conduct the weld test on Fridays, after first break, and there is a time limit. The time limit is adjusted for thicker plate and for larger diameter pipe. For the V-groove weld test, the three hold points are the same as for the fillet weld test, fit-up, root, and completed weld. On V-groove welds, the inspection is a two-part inspection: visual and destructive bend test.

The visual inspection for the V-groove only has seven items to inspect:

1) Excessive root reinforcement
2) Incomplete joint penetration
3) Excessive cap reinforcement
4) Porosity
5) Undercut
6) Under fill
7) Strike Marks

On the V-groove weld test, the starting grade is a 95, versus the 100 on the fillet weld test. I start the grade scale at 95 because I believe there is no perfect weld, especially in the training phase. Each of the items checked on the visual inspection are worth 10 points and if a student gets three items marked, the student fails the visual inspection and receives a grade of 65. If a student fails visual inspection that student does not cut and bend the weld test.

If a student gets two items or less marked on the visual inspection, the student gets to do the bend test. The bend test follows the AWS D1.1, for plate or ASME section IX for pipe, for the cutting of bend strips and criteria for passing. If a student's bend strips do not pass the bend test, they get a grade of 65. For one of my students to get a passing grade on a V-groove weld test in my program, a student's weld must pass the visual inspection with no more than two discontinuities and pass the bend test according to the applicable code. This is a tall order for someone new to welding, but it is easier than a weld test for a job because on a weld test for a job a weld can have no visual discontinuities and pass a bend test. The system I have gives my students a little leeway on the visual and a chance to learn how to take a weld test.

The only way to learn how to weld is to weld. The only way to teach someone to weld is to be beside them while they weld. You cannot teach someone to weld sitting in your office. I have seen plenty of welding instructors trying to teach from their office. It does not work. You have to be in the shop with your students observing what they are doing and giving them guidance.

When I am in the shop observing and helping my students, I get into what I call my "Great White Shark" mode. I put on my welding hood and I just cruise looking for a student to help. I will stick my head into their booths while they are welding to see how they are doing. Sometimes I let them know I am in the booth with them and sometimes I don't. I can get a more accurate assessment of what the student is doing if they don't know I'm in the booth with them. This gives me a true look at how they are welding. If they know I am in the booth with them before they start to weld, the student changes how they act and weld. If all of my students are doing well and no one needs my assistance, I stay in the shop, available and ready to help as soon as someone calls on me. I do my office work at the end of the day after the students have left.

The office is a necessary evil in technical education. We, as instructors, have to complete paperwork required by the school's administration. We have to order materials and keep up with the grades of our students. There is a lot of paperwork involved with a technical program. Don't let the paperwork overwhelm you or get you down. I personally hate doing paperwork. If I wanted to do paperwork for a living, I would have been an accountant or something like that, but I became a welder because I like working with my hands and paperwork is not working with your hands. If you need help with the office paperwork, ask for help. Don't wait until you are behind and get into trouble for not turning in information for a report. Most technical divisions have an administrative assistant that can give you guidance. Ask for help! Don't be the instructor who never turns in administrative work because you hate paperwork. Learn to deal with it. It's no fun, but you have to get it done.

Chapter 7

Training Aids and Budget

One of the reasons my students usually do well on the company's weld test is that I get my students out of their weld booths and have them weld in real life situations. I have built a couple of different job simulation areas at my shop. One we call "The Sandlot." It is basically a pipe rack built on some 12-inch I-beams sitting on the ground. The Sandlot requires the students to get on the ground and crawl under the pipes to weld. I make the students wear a reflective vest and harness while welding on the Sandlot. Why do I make my students weld in a harness if they are on the ground? To get them used to working in a harness and welding in one. Also, my students cannot use any of the shop equipment to prep any of their weld coupons for the Sandlot. I make the students treat the Sandlot like a job site and they can only use tools that they would have on a job site.

I also have the "Welder's Playground." This is a job simulation platform I built with material donated by a local company. It has a platform at 3-feet that is made of grating from an industrial plant. There is another platform at the top of the Playground at 15-feet above the ground. All platforms have OSHA compliant handrails and toe boards. Plus, I make the students use fall protection harnesses and lanyards when they are working on the Playground. Again, the students can only use tools that would be on a job site.

I use the "Sandlot" and "Playground" to teach different aspects of construction work, like fall protection and pipe fitting, but the main purpose of these job simulation areas is to get the students out of the weld booth. A student can be a great booth welder, but can they weld in the "real world"? The only way to find out is to get them out of the booth and put them into real world situations. You don't need a fancy "Playground" or "Sandlot" to do this. Just make up some sort of jig or stand that the students can weld in that is more of a challenge than the booth welding.

Budget

When it comes to the budget for a welding program, you may not have a lot of say in what the school gives you, but I am going to tell you what numbers I have found work for my programs. For a well-equipped welding program, I have found that the program needs a budget that works out to $675 per student, per semester. That is approximately $2,000 per student for a three-semester school year. My program is a year-round program that includes the summer. If your program does not include summers, you can adjust this dollar amount accordingly. According to these numbers, my program's budget for 30 students is $60,000 a year. That looks like a lot of money, but it costs a lot to run a welding program, and that is where a lot of schools get into trouble. Administrators do not understand the cost of running a welding program. The administration sees these numbers and thinks there is no way we can give that kind of money to one program, but the school, at least at the college level, can charge lab fees. That is where the schools I have taught at in the past have raised the money for the welding budget.

A school has to be careful not to charge too much or the students will not be able to afford the program. But the school should charge enough to cover the cost of the program and make it to where the students have a little skin in the game, so to speak. I believe you get what you pay for. If the price of the welding program is to cheap, there will not be a sufficient budget to operate the welding program. You, as the instructor, will be having to beg for scrap metal from businesses so that there is metal for the students to weld. Equipment will not be able to get repaired because there is no money in the budget for it. It is not a good situation to be in, I know, I've been there. But if the school can charge adequate lab fees to increase the budget, the welding program will be a better program. There will be money to buy metal, to repair equipment, and to buy welding rods. No matter what your budget is, you have to spend it wisely. Don't just buy something because it looks cool or is supposedly the latest and greatest. Make sure whatever you purchase, it is needed and adds value to your welding program.

At the college I am teaching at currently, I have blanket purchase orders (P.O.) for welding gases and welding supplies at two different weld supply companies. The blanket p.o. is for a certain amount for the year. Having a blanket p.o. is nice. I know how much I have to spend and all I have to do is call up the supply company and order materials. I suggest working with your administration to let you set up blanket p.o.'s to your weld suppliers.

I have to be careful not to go over the p.o. amount. I did this once and only once. It was not a pretty picture. The accounts payable personnel at my school made sure I understood that this was not to happen again. So, to keep from over-spending again, I set up an expense tracking system using an Excel spreadsheet. I use this tracking system to show how much of the p.o. I have spent and how much I have left to spend. This expense tracking system has been a life saver. It has kept me out trouble.

Chapter 8

Getting Students Hired

Once you have recruited the students and trained the students, now it is time to help the students get hired. By state law, I cannot guarantee a job to a student, but I do my best to give them an opportunity at a job before they finish the last semester of the welding program. I do this a couple of different ways. The first is to have a strong advisory committee. Most schools and colleges will require you to have two advisory committee meetings a year. I hold mine in the Spring and Fall semesters. The Spring semester meeting is for the local businesses that use welders and have hired or might hire some of my graduates. This advisory meeting is usually small, maybe 3 or 4 welding businesses, and my weld supply company representative. I hold my advisory meetings in the afternoon at 4:30pm on a Tuesday, Wednesday, or Thursday. Mondays I feel are too hectic, and nobody wants to go to a meeting on Friday afternoon after work. This time, and the days, works good for my members because it is right at the end of the work day, so they can leave the meeting and go home.

Having an advisory meeting for the local businesses helps me keep up with their needs and keeps me honed in on what changes or tweaks might need to be made to the welding program. Make sure you take good notes on what this advisory committee suggests because those suggestions can guide your program goals for the next year.

The Fall advisory committee meeting is the big one. I invite every business I know from everywhere. I have had company representatives fly in from out of state to attend this meeting. This Fall meeting is a regional advisory committee meeting I started because my students were not getting jobs locally. Most of my students were getting jobs with construction companies and these companies were sending my students across the Southeast to do work. This large meeting has helped give me and my program credibility with my college's administration. Make sure you have a good advisory committee. They can help you more than you know.

Another way I help to get my students opportunities for jobs is to have weld test days. I set up a couple of days a year for different companies to send their weld inspectors to my shop and give weld tests to my graduating students. I usually have 2 or 3 companies come on the same day. I make sure everyone from the different companies are comfortable with this, and it has not created any problems thus far.

These weld test days really help the students get hired because if a student passes a weld test for one of the companies, that student's name goes on the company's hire list. When a job comes open that requires a certain weld certification which the student holds, the company gives them a call with a job offer. Some of my students have passed weld tests for several companies and had multiple job offers before they finished the program. The test days have been very beneficial to my students and my program because they have helped get students jobs and it lets me see what the company inspectors are looking for as an acceptable weld. With this knowledge, I can better train my other students to be prepared for their weld test days the following year.

Chapter 9

Welding Competitions

Most school administrators like to see their school getting positive press coverage at the local and national levels. One of the best ways to do this is to participate in welding competitions. The most known welding competition is SkillsUSA. This is a national organization that has regional and state welding competitions that can lead to the national competition. I think SkillsUSA is a great organization for high school welding students. It lets them see that welding is a big world with all sorts of different people and different career paths. I do not think SkillsUSA is a good organization for the college level student because SkillsUSA focuses on fabrication and metal art. SkillsUSA does not have a segment in the welding competition for construction structural welding or pipe welding. And since I don't teach fabrication, I do not see the value in SkillsUSA for my students. Plus, SkillsUSA is an extracurricular activity which means me and the students involved would have to spend more time at the school preparing for the competition. As I said earlier, most of my students work night and weekend jobs, so staying after school or coming in on weekends is really not an option for them.

One welding competition I do like is the Associated Builders and Contractors (ABC) Craft Championships. This competition is about construction trades. The welding competition is for structural welding and pipe welding. This competition is based on the NCCER curriculum and since I teach that in my shop, I don't have to spend time outside of my normal work hours to get my students ready. This competition is a national competition held once a year. The welding competition winner gets a gold medal, a cash prize, a MIG welder, and a trip to Washington D.C. to attend a Washington Nationals baseball game, where the winners from all the Craft Championship contests will be recognized in a pre-game ceremony.

Both of these organizations, SkillsUSA and ABC Craft Championships, are good organizations to join. You need to see if either of them fit your program and would help expose your students to the bigger world of welding. There are some costs involved with competing in these organizations, so you will need to factor that in with your decision, but don't let money stop you from taking your students to these competitions. The experience they get will be well worth the price, in my opinion.

Conclusion

I know not everyone teaches the same way and what works for one person may not work for the other. The things I do may not work for you, but I hope that seeing how I teach welding inspires you to come up with your own ideas of how to teach better. Good luck and Light'em up!!

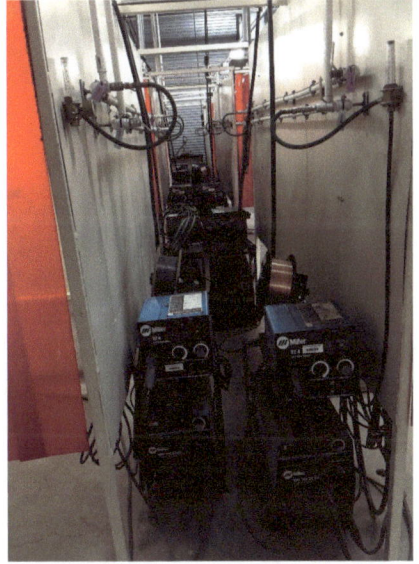

"Alley" between weld booths for welding machines

Sandlot Jobsite Simulator

The Welder's Playground job site simulator

Appendices:

WELD SHOP RULES AND DRESS CODE

You are adults and are expected to behave like adults.

Safety is paramount and will be monitored at all times.

1. No profanity tolerated.
2. No sexual, racial, or ethnic jokes.
3. No horseplay.
4. Class starts promptly at 7:15 a.m. Monday thru Friday.
   Students will come to class dressed and prepared to weld.
5. Class ends at 3:00 p.m. Monday thru Friday.
6. Absenteeism will not be tolerated.
   If you miss more than 10% of class time you will receive a grade of F in accordance with the program attendance policy.

   > Fall Semester: Maximum absences is 6
   > Being tardy to class = 1 unexcused absence
   > 2 Early outs = 1 unexcused absence (leaving before the
   >   scheduled end of a class period or before the instructor
   >   releases the class)

7. If, in the opinion of an instructor, you are not in a state to safely work in the weld shop, you will be asked to leave and it will count as an unexcused absence for that day.
8. Tennis shoes <u>WILL NOT</u> be tolerated in the welding shop <u>AT ANY TIME</u>. **Only** ankle high <u>steel-toed boots</u> may be worn.
9. **<u>Clear safety glasses will be worn at ALL TIMES in the welding shop.</u>**
10. A clear face shield, ear plugs, and gloves will be worn when using a grinder and/or equipment that produces sparks.
11. Gloves will be worn while welding, grinding, or handling metal.
12. A #5 tinted face shield will be worn when using cutting equipment.
13. If tee shirts are worn, they will have 4" or longer sleeve.
14. There will no obscene or offensive pictures or wording on clothing, equipment, or tools. This includes stickers or writing on welding hoods or tool boxes.
15. No permanent press or synthetic fibers (polyester) clothing allowed. Clothing is to be 100% cotton or denim and be properly fitted (no baggy pants).
16. No jewelry is to be worn in the welding shop or classroom (medical emergency jewelry, exempted).
17. Each student is responsible for his/her own tools and should have them properly marked.

18. <u>ALL buildings on college campuses are tobacco free.</u>
      <u>NO</u> tobacco use except in designated areas.
      <u>NO</u> tobacco products on your person at any time
          while in the welding shop or classroom.
19. **<u>No cell phones, radios, or other such electronic devices are allowed in shop or classroom at any time.</u>**

1st Violation: leave class or shop and **<u>unexcused</u>** absence for that day. Repeated violations of the conduct, safety and dress code will be reported to the appropriate school authorities for disciplinary action. Please refer to the conduct element of the Student Handbook found online for any questions about school conduct or dress code.

Welding Office Phone number: xxx-xxx-xxxx

Summer Semester				
Pipe Lecture / Test Schedule				
	Date		Book	Chap
Thur	June 14	Lecture -SMAW Carbon Steel Pipe	LVL 3	1
Tues	June 19	*Test -SMAW C.S. Pipe*		
Thur	June 21	Lecture - GMAW Pipe	LVL 3	2
Tues	June 26	*Test - GMAW Pipe*		
Thur	June 28	Lecture - FCAW Pipe	LVL 3	3
Tues	July 3	*Test - FCAW Pipe*		
Thur	July 5	Lecture - GTAW Carbon Steel Pipe	LVL 3	4
Tues	July 17	*Test - GTAW Carbon Steel Pipe*		
Thur	July 19	Lecture - GTAW S. S. Pipe	LVL 3	5
Tues	July 24	*Test - GTAW S.S. Pipe*		
Thur	July 26	Lecture - SMAW - S.S. Groove Welds	LVL 3	6
Tues	July 31	*Test - SMAW -S.S. Groove Welds*		

Pipe Weld Test Schedule

Date	Weld Test
Combo (TIG & Stick)	
Aug 24	6" - 2G - Pad
Aug 31	6" - 2G
Sept 7	6" - 6G - Pad
Sept 14	6" - 6G
Sept 21	6" - 5G - Pad
Sept 28	6" - 5G
Oct 5	2" - 2G
Oct 12	2" - 6G
Oct 19	2" - 5G
Stainless Steel	
Oct 26	2" - 2G
Nov 2	2" - 6G
Nov 9	2" - 5G
Nov 16	2" - 6G - Sch. 10
Bi - Metal	
Nov 30	2" - 6G
Combo (TIG & Stick)	
Dec 7	2" Monster - 6G

Date	Weld Test (cont'd.)
Dec 13	2" Monster TIG out - 6G

SMAW (Stick) Weld Test Schedule

Date	Weld Test
Aug 31	7018 - 1F Pad *(Not Graded)*
Sept 7	7018 - 2F Pad *(Not Graded)*
Sept 14	7018 - 2F Tee
Sept 21	7018 - 2F Lap
Sept 28	7018 - 3F Tee
Oct 5	7018 - 4F Tee
Oct 12	*6010 - 1F & 2F Pad (Not Graded)*
Oct 19	*6010 - 2F Tee*
Oct 26	*6010 - 3F Tee*
Nov 2	*6010 - 4F Tee*
Nov 9	7018 - 3G - 3/8" Plate w/ Back Strip
Nov 16	7018 - 4G - 3/8" Plate w/ Back Strip
Nov 30	7018 - 3G - 1" Plate w/ Back Strip
Dec 7	7018 - 4G - 1" Plate w/ Back Strip

Date	Weld Test (Cont'd)
Dec 13	oxy/fuel cutting project

Weld Test Materials Specifications

- All lap joints test will be on ¼" material that is 2" x 6"

- Lap joint test will be single beads on both sides of the material. The student picks which side is to be graded.

- T joints for 6010, GMAW and GTAW will be on ¼" material that is 2" x 6".

- T joints for 7018 will be on 3/8" material that is 12" x 3". 7018 – 1/8" welding rods will be used for these T joints.

- T joint test will have a single bead on one side and three beads on the other side (root /2 cover beads).

- Groove test with backing stripe, will be on 3/8" plate that is 6" x 4" or 1" plate that is 6"x 4".

- The backing stripe will be ¼" material between 1" – 2" wide and 8" long.

- Open butt groove weld test for 6010/7018 will be on 3/8" plate that is 12"x4".

- Open butt groove weld test for GMAW/GTAW will be on 3/8" plate that is 6" x 4".

- Students will stamp their welder I.D.# and weld position on each test. For lap joints the student's welder I.D. # and position will be stamped on the side of the lap joint the student wants graded. For T-joints, welder I.D. # and position will be stamped on the single bead side, welder I.D. # on the left and weld position on the right.

- Weld test will be conducted on the last class day of the week after morning break.

Guidelines for Administering a Fillet Weld Test

> Once the test plates are tacked together, students will stamp their welder I.D. # (last 4 of their student I.D. number) on the left side of the fillet weld test plate.

>Students will stamp the position number (1, 2, 3, 4) for the position the test will be taken in on the right-side fillet weld test plate.

>Once weld test coupon is tacked in position, the instructor shall verify that the weld coupon is in the proper position.

>NO grinding shall be done on the fillet weld test. Cleaning of the weld beads should be done with a chipping hammer, wire brush, or power brush.

>The instructor will conduct a visual inspection of the weld using the following criteria:

- Uniform rippled appearance
- Craters and restarts filled to the full cross section of the weld
- Uniform weld size ± 1/16
- Smooth flat transition w/ complete fusion at the toe of the weld
- Acceptable weld profile in accordance with D1.1
- No porosity
- No undercut
- No cold lap
- No strike marks
- Good visual appearance.

- ○ 6 points will be subtracted from the student's grade for each area from the above list that has a discontinuity.

Plate Weld Test Guidelines

Plate weld test with backing strip shall follow AWS D1.1 - Structural Welding Code - Steel

- Weld test plates shall have a 22 ½ degree bevel for an inclusive angle of 45 degrees
- The root opening shall be ¼".
- Once tacked together, the student shall stamp their welder I.D. # on the left side of the backing strip on the test plate.
- Students shall stamp the position in which the test is welded on the right side of the backing strip on the test plate.
- Once weld test plate is tacked in position, the instructor shall verify that the weld coupon is within AWS tolerances for that position.
- The weld test plate shall NOT be moved for any reason once the instructor has approved its positioning until the finished weld is visually verified by the instructor
- The root weld bead and filler beads should be cleaned with chipping hammer, wire brush, power brush, or grinder as necessary.
- NO grinding shall be done on the cap pass. Cleaning of the cap pass should be done with a wire brush or power brush.
- Plate weld test will have time limits.
  - 3/8" plate - 60 min
  - 1" plate - 120 min

- When a student has completed a plate weld test, the instructor shall check to make sure the plate was not moved during the welding of the test.
- The instructor shall perform a visual inspection using the following guidelines:

  - Weld reinforcement shall not exceed 1/8" above base metal
  - The face of the weld shall be a minimum of flush with the base metal
  - No visible porosity
  - No Undercut
  - No cold lap
  - There shall be no strike marks on the face of the weld plate outside the weld zone

- Bend test specimens shall be cut from the test plate in accordance with AWS D1.1. See Figure 2.
- Have the student lay out bend specimen in the following manner:

  - Find and mark center line of the test plate along the 6" side
  - Measure and mark 1" on both sides of center line
  - Measure and mark 1 ½" from the 1" marks
  - The 1 ½" strips are the bend specimens

- The student shall stamp their welder I.D. # on the back of each bend specimen along the right side and the position of the test along the left side.
- Once the bend specimens are cut, the student shall remove the backing strip and weld reinforcement from the face of the weld.
- The corners of the specimen should be rounded to a 1/16" radius
- Once the bend specimens are properly prepared, the   instructor will bend the specimens and inspect the   specimens in accordance with AWS D1.1.

For 3/8" plate
- One specimen will be bent to show the face of the weld.
- One specimen will be bent to show the root of the weld.

For 1" plate
- Two specimens will be bent to show side profile of the weld.

Acceptance criteria for bend specimens

- The surface of the bend specimen shall have no discontinuities that exceed 1/8" in any direction
- Corner cracks shall not exceed ¼" except when there is visible slag inclusions then the 1/8" maximum shall apply.
- Add together the measurements of all discontinuities that exceed 1/32" but are smaller than or equal 1/8". The total shall not exceed 1/8".

Grading Scale for plate weld test

0 visual defects and pass the bend test - 95
1 visual defects and pass the bend test - 85
2 visual defects and pass the bend test - 75
If 3 visual defects - 65
Fail Face or Root bend - 65

Pipe Weld Test Guidelines

1. Pipe weld tests will have time limits.

    •   2" pipe tests will be limited to 90 minutes.

    •   4" pipe tests will be limited to 2 ½ hours.

    •   6" pipe tests will be limited to 4 hours.

    •   Any student who does not finish the weld test within the set time limit fails the weld test and must reschedule the weld test with the instructor.

2. Students will stamp their welder I.D. # on the pipe coupons at the top of the pipe at the 12 o'clock position after the pipe test is tacked together but before beginning the weld test.

3. Once the weld test is tacked in position, the instructor shall verify that the weld coupon is within code tolerances for that position.

4. The weld test coupon shall NOT be moved for any reason once the instructor has approved its positioning until the finished weld is visually verified by the instructor.

5. The instructor will do a visual inspection of the root pass before the student continues with the weld test.

6. The root weld bead and filler beads should be cleaned with the chipping hammer, the wire brush, the power brush, or the grinder as necessary.

7. NO grinding shall be done on the cap pass. Cleaning of the cap pass should be done with a wire brush or power brush.

8. The instructor shall perform a visual inspection using the following guidelines:

   - Weld root reinforcement shall not exceed 1/16"

   - Weld root shall be a minimum of flush with the base metal

   - Weld face reinforcement shall not exceed 1/8" above base metal

   - The face of the weld shall be a minimum of flush with the base metal

   - No visible porosity

   - Undercut shall not exceed 1/32" in depth

   - No cold lap

   - There shall be no strike marks on the face of the weld coupon outside the weld zone

9. Once student has welded the coupon and the instructor has visually inspected and passed the pipe weld, the student is ready to cut bend strips.

10. The student will lay out the bend strips according to appropriate pipe weld code (ASME Section IX).

11. Once the student has cut the bend strips, the student will stamp on the root side of the strips their welder I.D. # on the left side of the strip and the position number for the position the test was taken in on the right side of the strip before grinding and cleaning of the bend strip.

12. The bend specimen shall not have any discontinuity larger than 1/8" in any direction.

Grading Scale for plate weld test

   0 visual defect and pass the bend test – 95
   1 visual defect and pass the bend test – 85

2 visual defects and pass the bend test - 75
If 3 visual defects - 65 or retake weld test
Fail Face or Root bend - 65 or retake weld test

Weld Test Grade Sheet

Name:	Welder I.D. #

Date of Test: Module #:	NCCER

Fillet Weld Visual Inspection		Groove Weld Bend Test	
Base Metal Thickness:	**Filler:**	**Base Metal:**	**Filler:**
1/4" 3/8"	GMAW 7018 GTAW 6010 E71T-1 ER309	Plate Time Pipe Time 3/8" 45mins. 2" 90mins. 1" 2 hours. 6" 2.5 hrs.	ER70-S(MIG) 7018 ER70-S(TIG) 6010 E71T-1 ER309
Joint: Pad / Tee / Lap	**Position:** 1 2 3 4	**Backing:** With / Without	**Position:** 1 2 3 4 5 6
1) Uniform rippled appearance on bead face		**Visual Inspection** 1) Excessive reinforcement - Root	
2.) Craters and restarts filled to the full cross section of the weld		2) Incomplete Penetration	
3) Uniform weld size + 1/16		4) Excessive reinforcement - Cap	

4.) Complete fusion at the toe of the weld		**5)** Porosity	
5.) Acceptable weld profile in accordance with D1.1		**6)** Undercut	
6.) Porosity		**7)** Under Fill	
7.) Undercut		**8)** Strike marks	
8.) Cold lap		**Visual Inspection**	Pass Fail
9.) Strike marks		**Bend Results**	
10.) Visual appearance		Face / Side	Pass Fail
		Root / Side	Pass Fail
GRADE: **Hold points:**		**TIME:** **GRADE:** **Hold points:**	

Required Tools for Welding Program by weld process

New Student / Stick Tool Kit #1

Safety glasses - Clear	2 pair
Fiber Metal Pipeline Welding Helmet with ratchet head gear and #10 shade	1
Clear lenses – 2x4	6
Welding Gloves – heavy duty gauntlet style	2 pair
Leather work gloves (Driver's gloves)	2 pair
Chipping Hammer	1
Hand Wire Brush	1
Welding Coat with leather sleeves	1 - large
Welding Cap	1
Tape measure – 25'	1
Locking Pliers (vise grip pliers)	1
Flash Light	1
Tool bag	1

MIG & TIG Tool Kit #2

Welder Pliers	1
TIG welding gloves	1 pair
Lineman's Pliers (side cutters)	1
10" Adjustable Wrench	1
6" Adjustable Wrench	1
Tungsten – 2% Thoriated - 1/8"	1 box
Stainless steel hand bush	1
Small Tool bag	1

Stick Pipe Tool Kit #3

Stinger – 150 Amp electrode holder with 15 foot of #2 welding cable with Linco male quick disconnect	1
Hard Hat – Fiber Metal (blue)	1
Capmount adaptor - halo (welding hood to hard hat)	1
Welding Gloves – heavy duty gauntlet style	2 pair

Leather work gloves (Driver's gloves)

2 pair

Clear lenses – 2x4

6

File – Nicholson half round bastard

1

Tool bag

1

Advanced Pipe Tool Bucket - Kit #4

Inspection mirror – 1 ¼" round	1
TIG Rig w/ 25ft power cable / hose - 150-amp 17FV	
	1
150 Amp TIG Torch Extension Kit, Tweco/Lenco Type	
	1
Regulator / Flowmeter (Mickey Mouse ears style)	
	1
Gas hose	20 ft.
Collet body – jumbo gas lens – 1/8"	4
1/8" collet	5
2% Thoriated tungsten – 1/8"	1 box
Jumbo gas cup #10	10
Jumbo cup insulator	2
Tool bucket – 5 gallon	1

Scottie Smith's Biography

Scottie Smith has over 25 years of experience working in the welding industry. He has worked as a post-secondary welding instructor since 2009. Scottie's teaching has been recognized with numerous awards over the years, including the 2010 Welding Instructor of the Year by the American Welding Society District 9; 2011 Certified Welding Inspector of the Year by the American Welding Society District 9; 2015 national Howard E. Adkins Memorial Instructor Award. Scottie was also the recipient of the 2018 Dale P. Parnell Distinguished Faculty designation and was named the 2018 Instructor of the Year by *The Welder* magazine.

During his military service as a welder in the Navy, he received a Navy and Marine Corps Achievement Medal and a Navy Good Conduct Medal. Scottie received his Associate of Applied Science Degree in Welding Technology from Southern Union State Community College along with an Associate of Applied Science Degree in Fire Science from Chattahoochee Valley Community College. Scottie also holds national certifications from organizations such as the National Center for Construction Education and Research, the American Welding Society, and the Occupational Safety and Health Administration. During his college career, Scottie was inducted as a member of the Phi Theta Kappa International Honor Society and received his welding training from his father, Frank Smith, who also received the national Howard E. Adkins Memorial Instructor Membership Award in 1999.

Scottie has been employed as the welding instructor at Northwest Florida State College in Niceville, Florida, since 2013. Scottie was instrumental in the implementation and launch of the welding program at NWF State College under a grant from the U.S. Department of Labor. He helped build the welding lab from the ground up and has demonstrated the ability to effectively and efficiently develop a successful program under strict budget constraints.

In 2018, The Northwest Florida State College welding program received the Gold Level endorsement from the Central Gulf Industrial Alliance and was also the recipient of the Wemco Excellence in Welding Award for an Educational Institution. In March of 2019, Northwest Florida State College welding program passed an American Welding Society audit and was recommended to become an American Welding Society Accredited Testing Facility.

www.ingramcontent.com/pod-product-compliance
Lightning Source LLC
Chambersburg PA
CBHW040125270326
41926CB00001B/21